B!TCH SERIES

Amusing Swear Words To Color

For Stress Releasing

By

Queenie McJody

Happy Coloring!

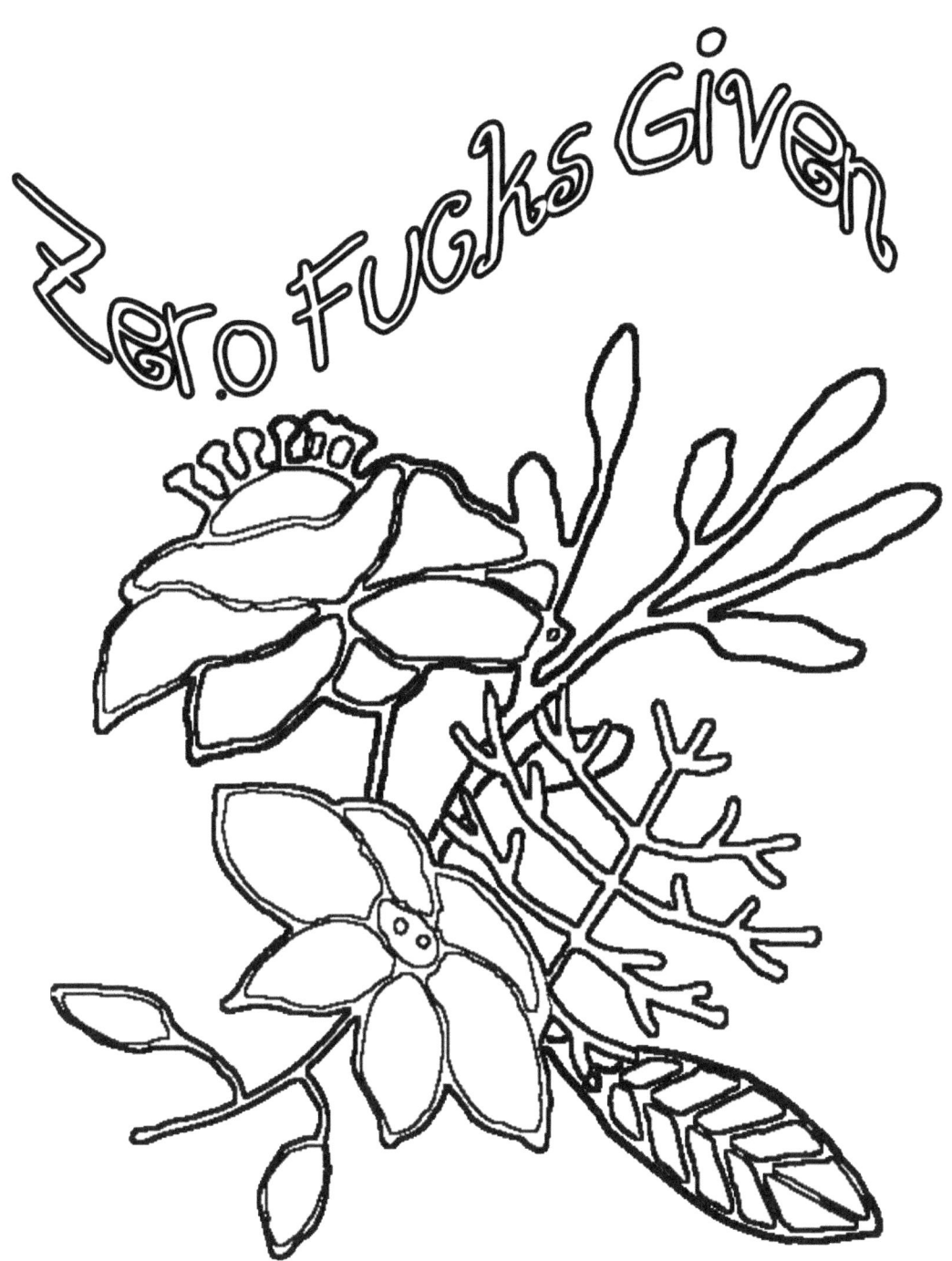

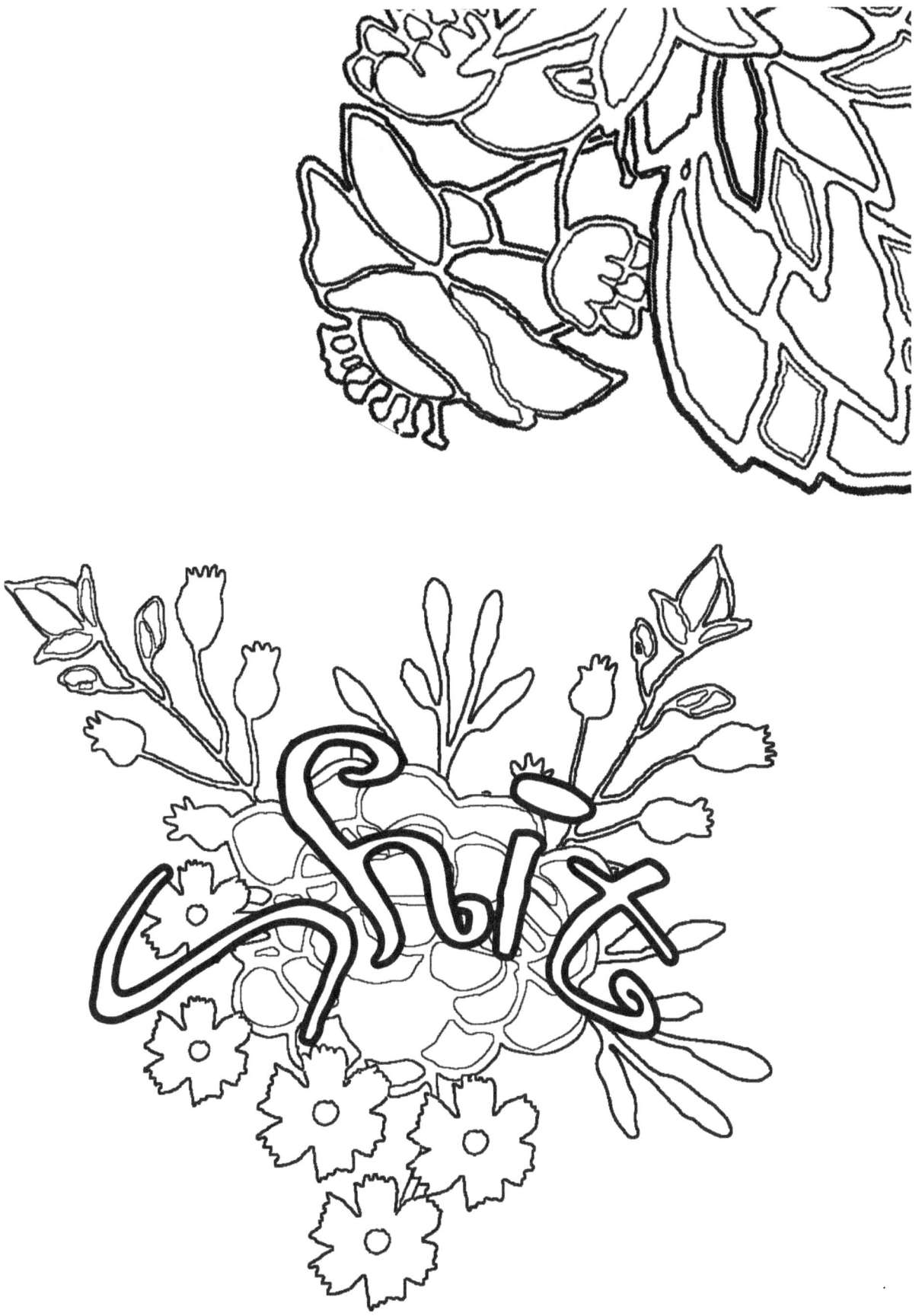

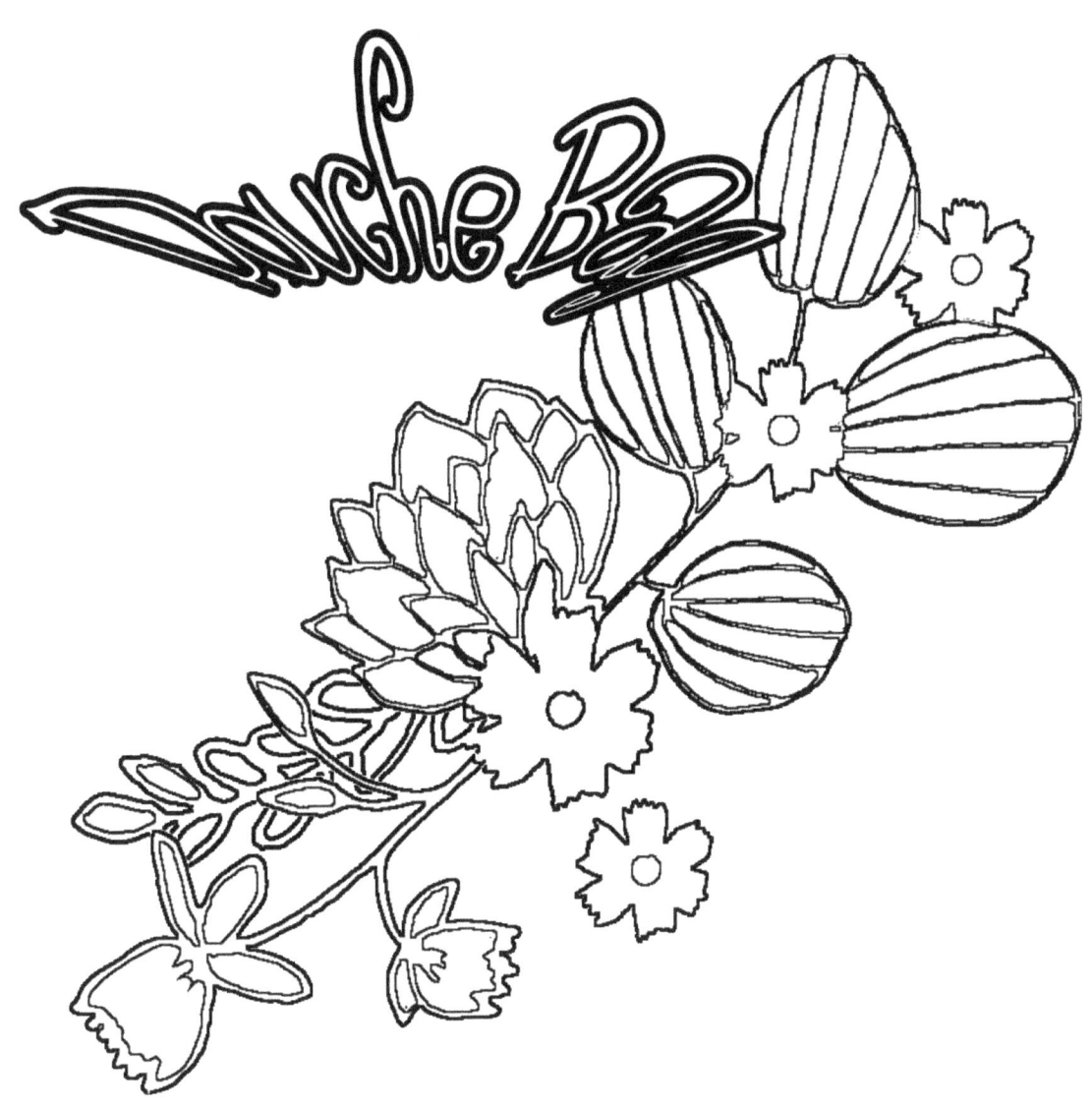

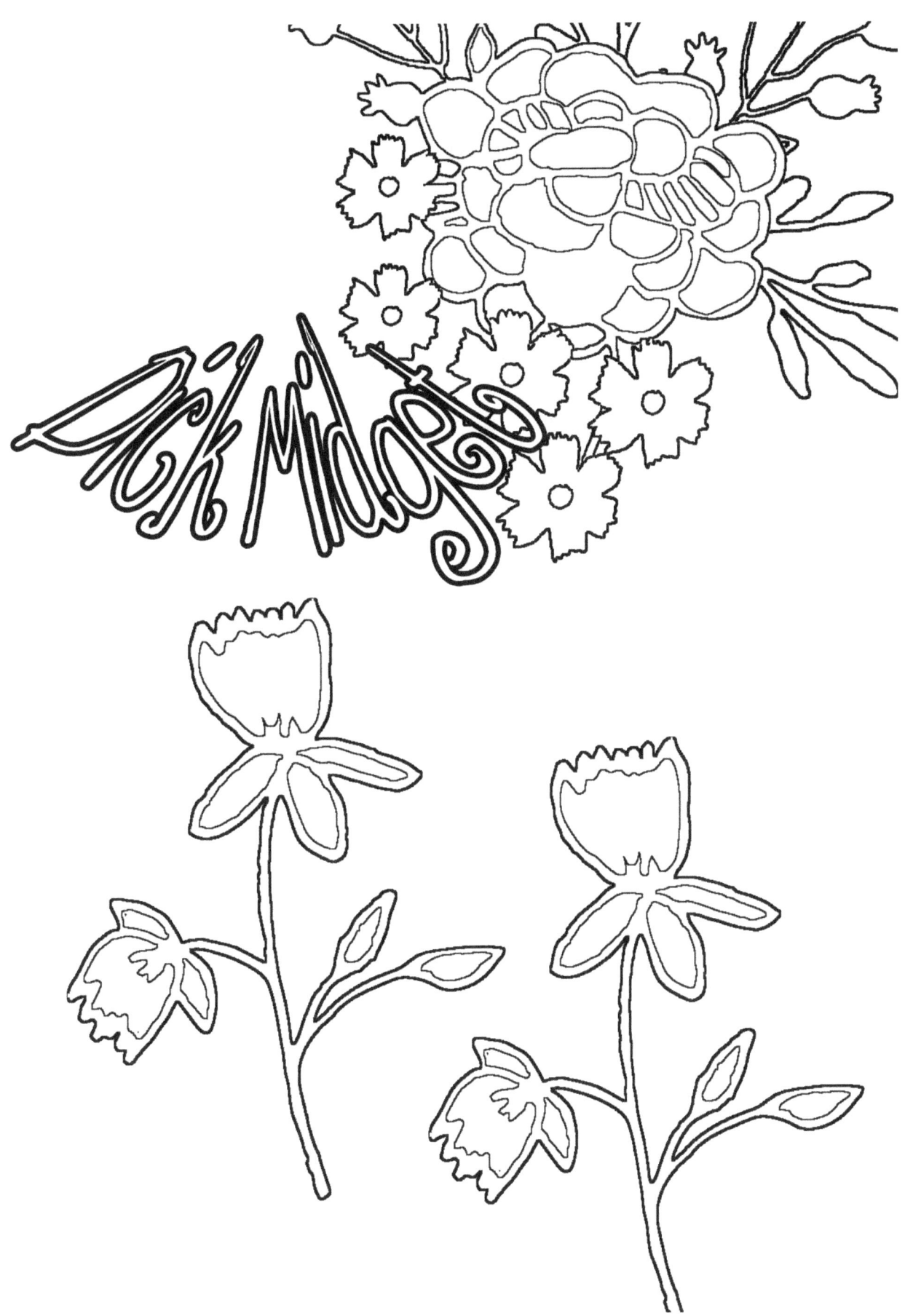

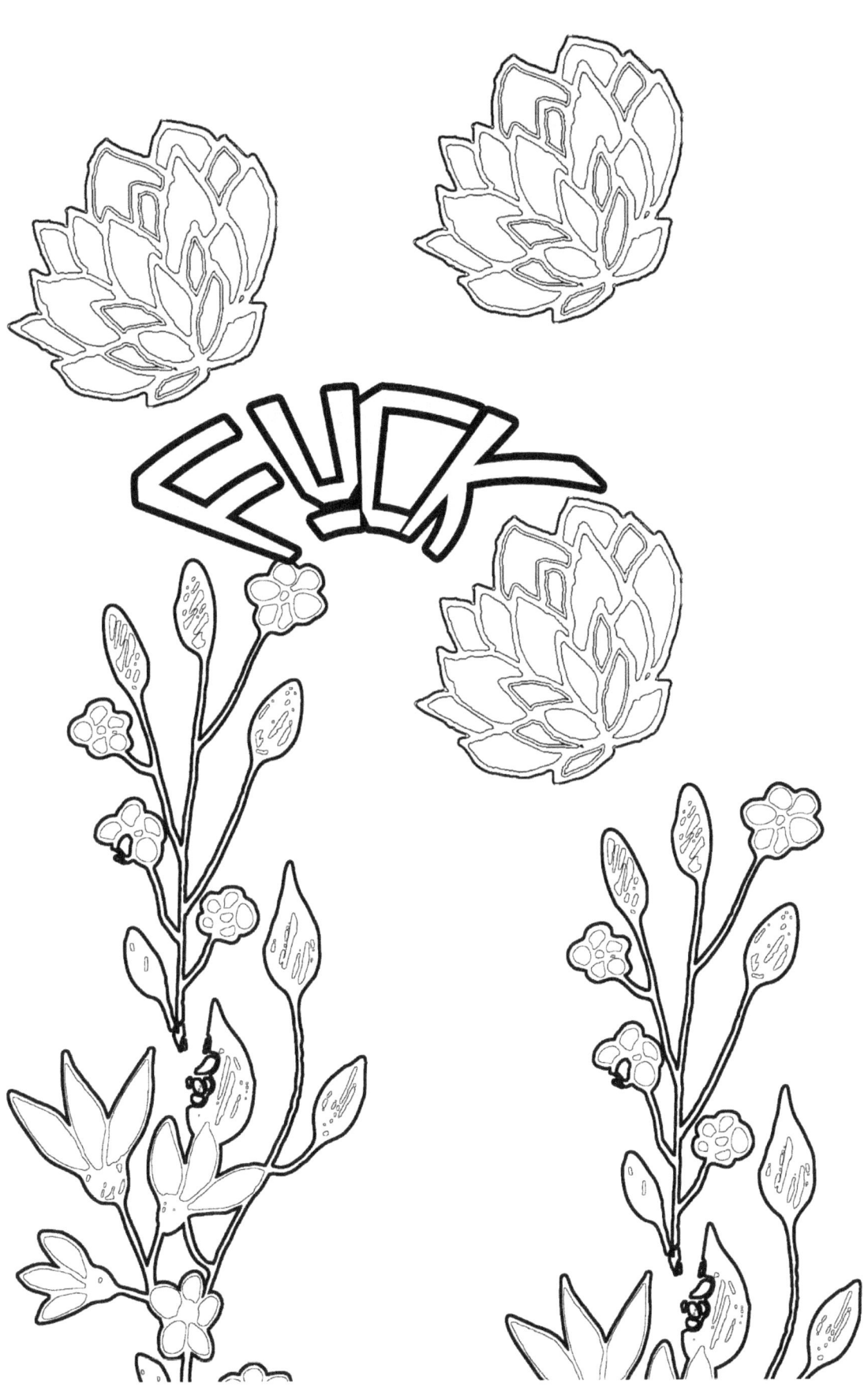

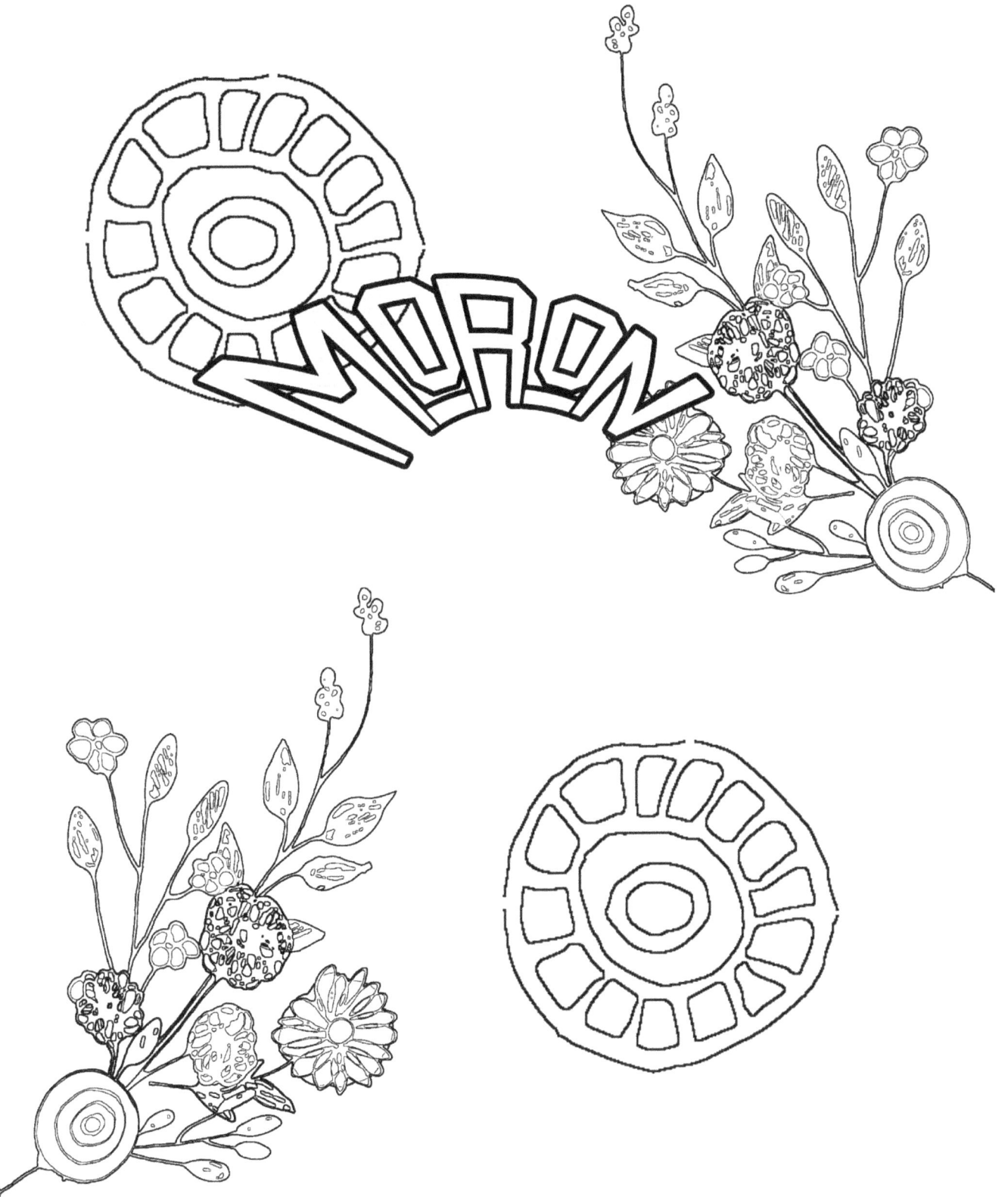

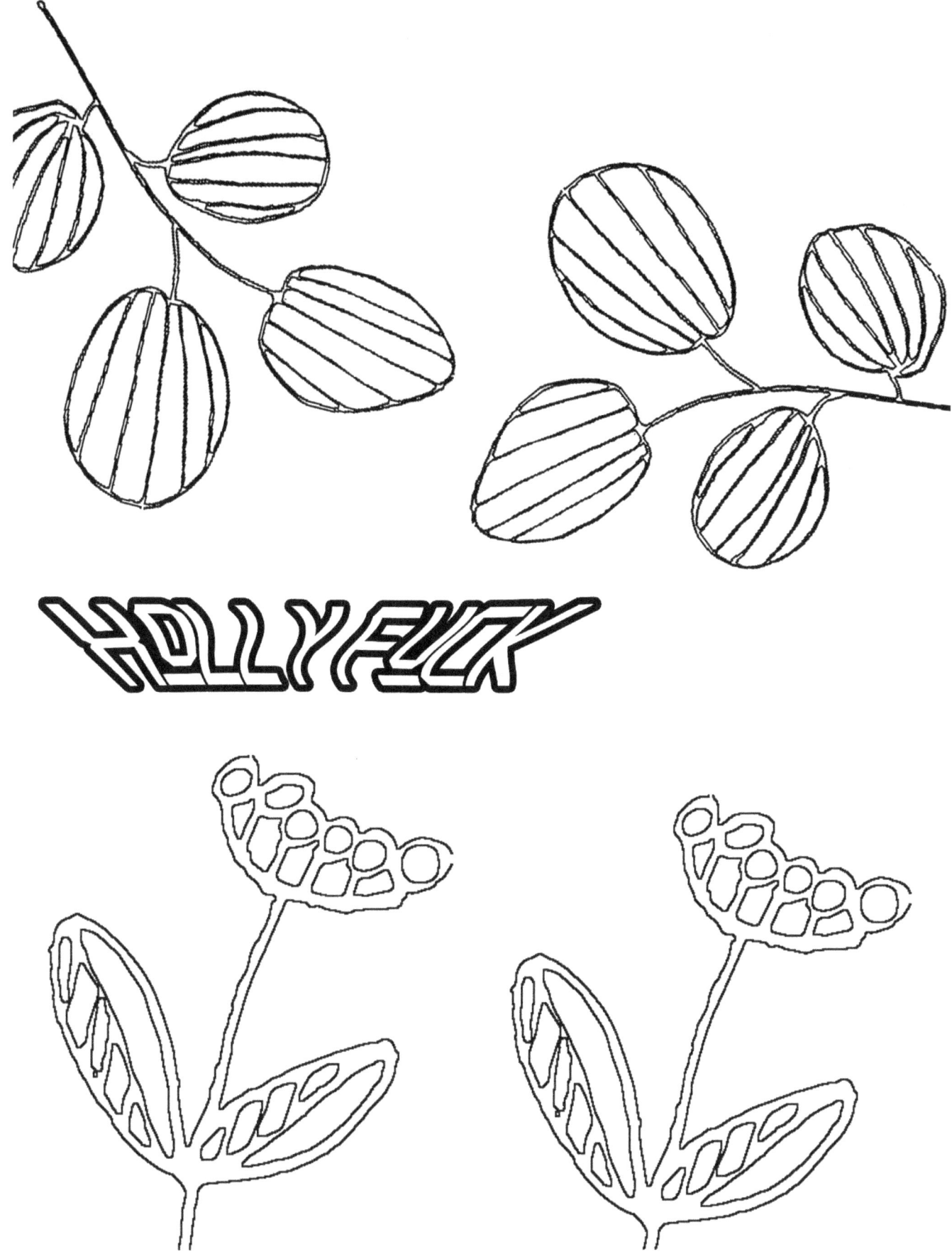

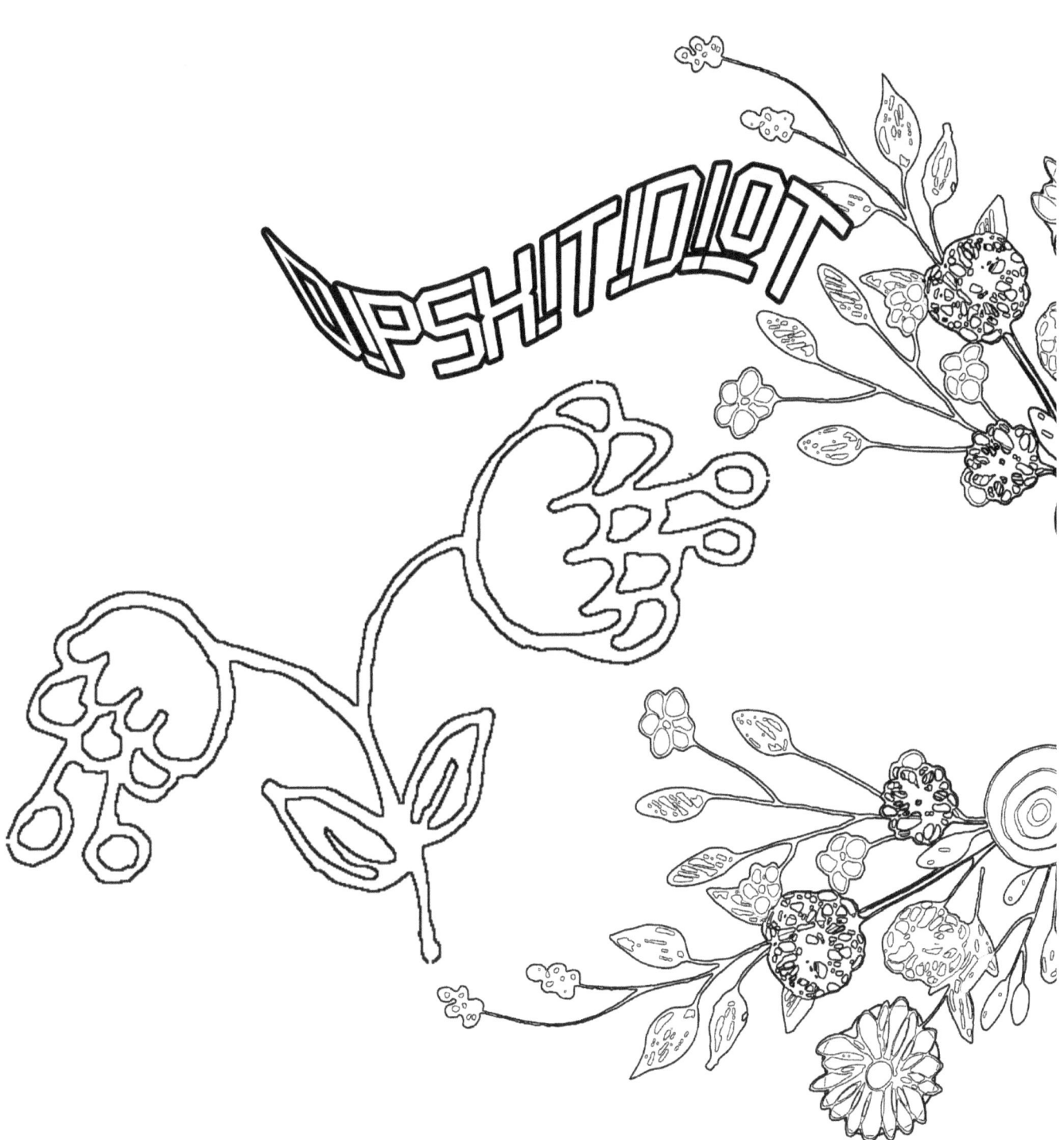

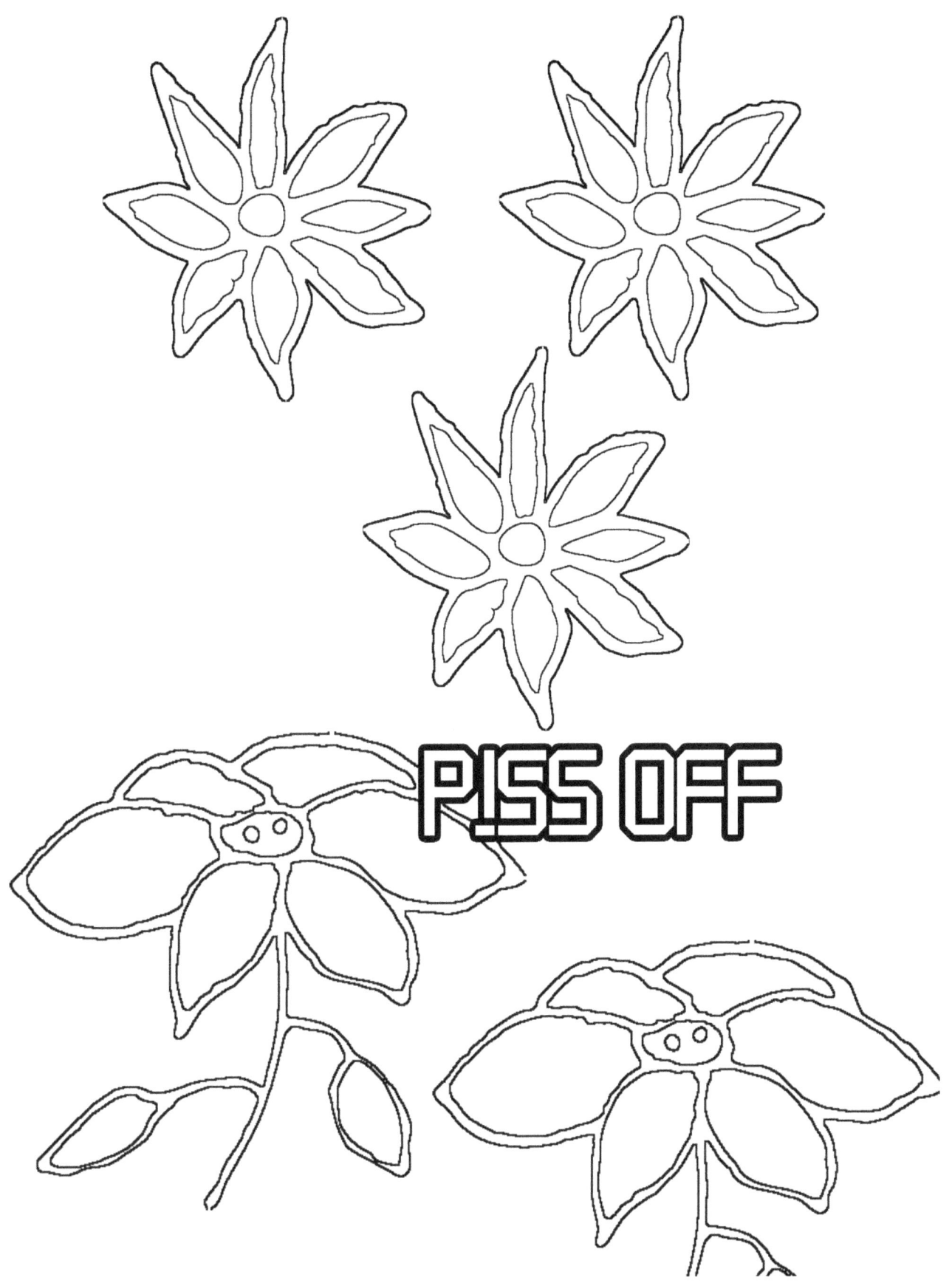

PISS OFF

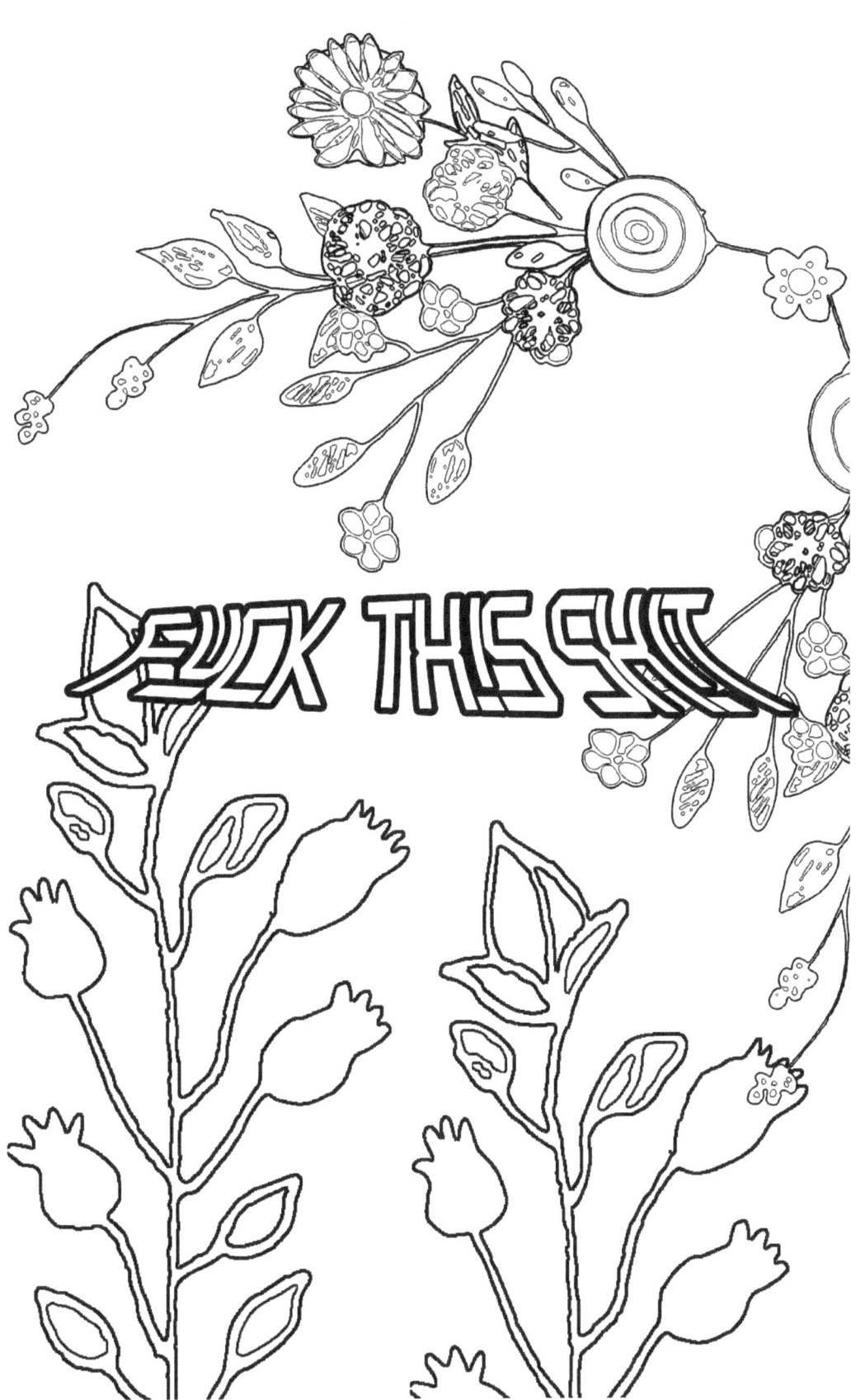

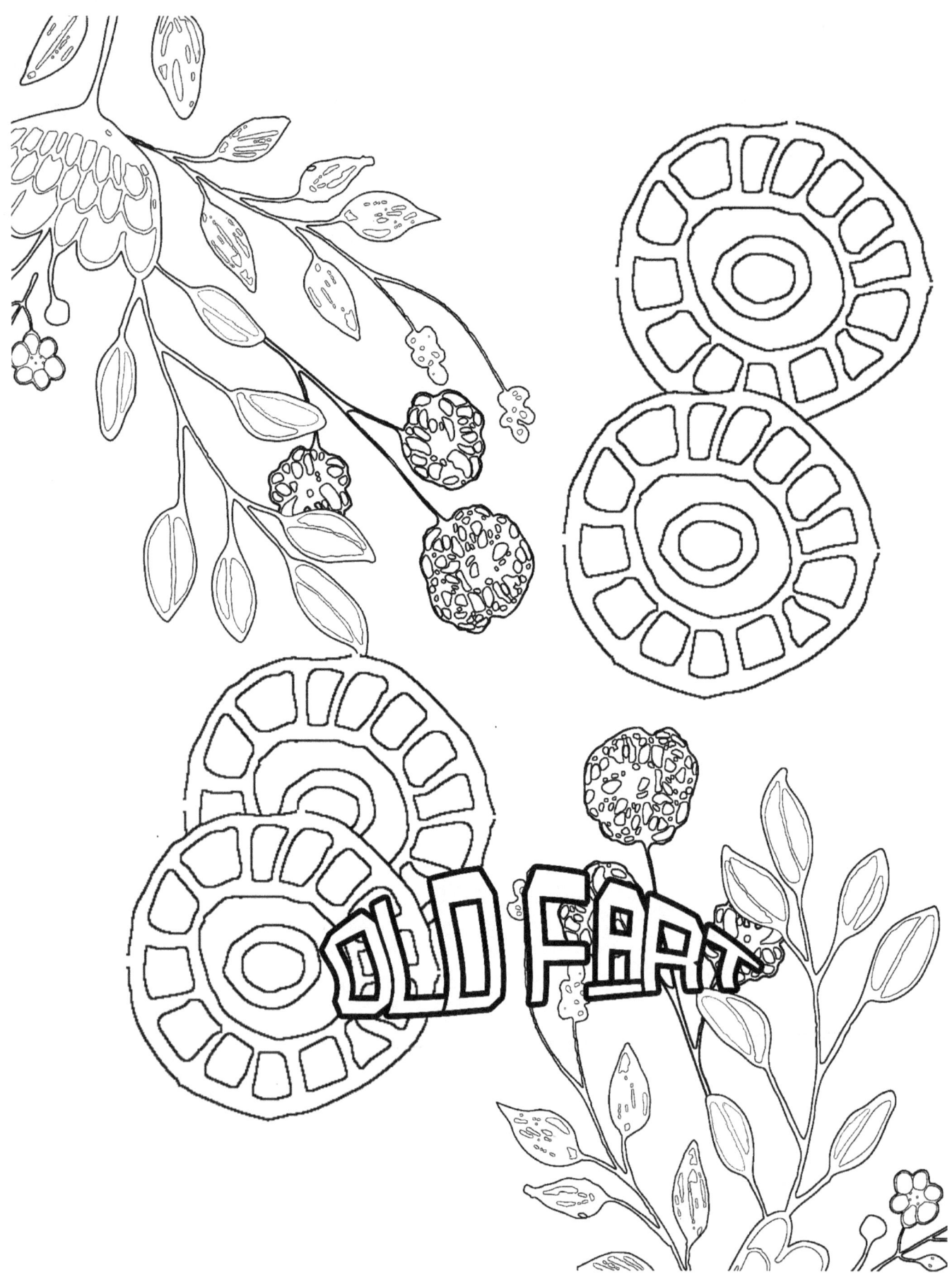

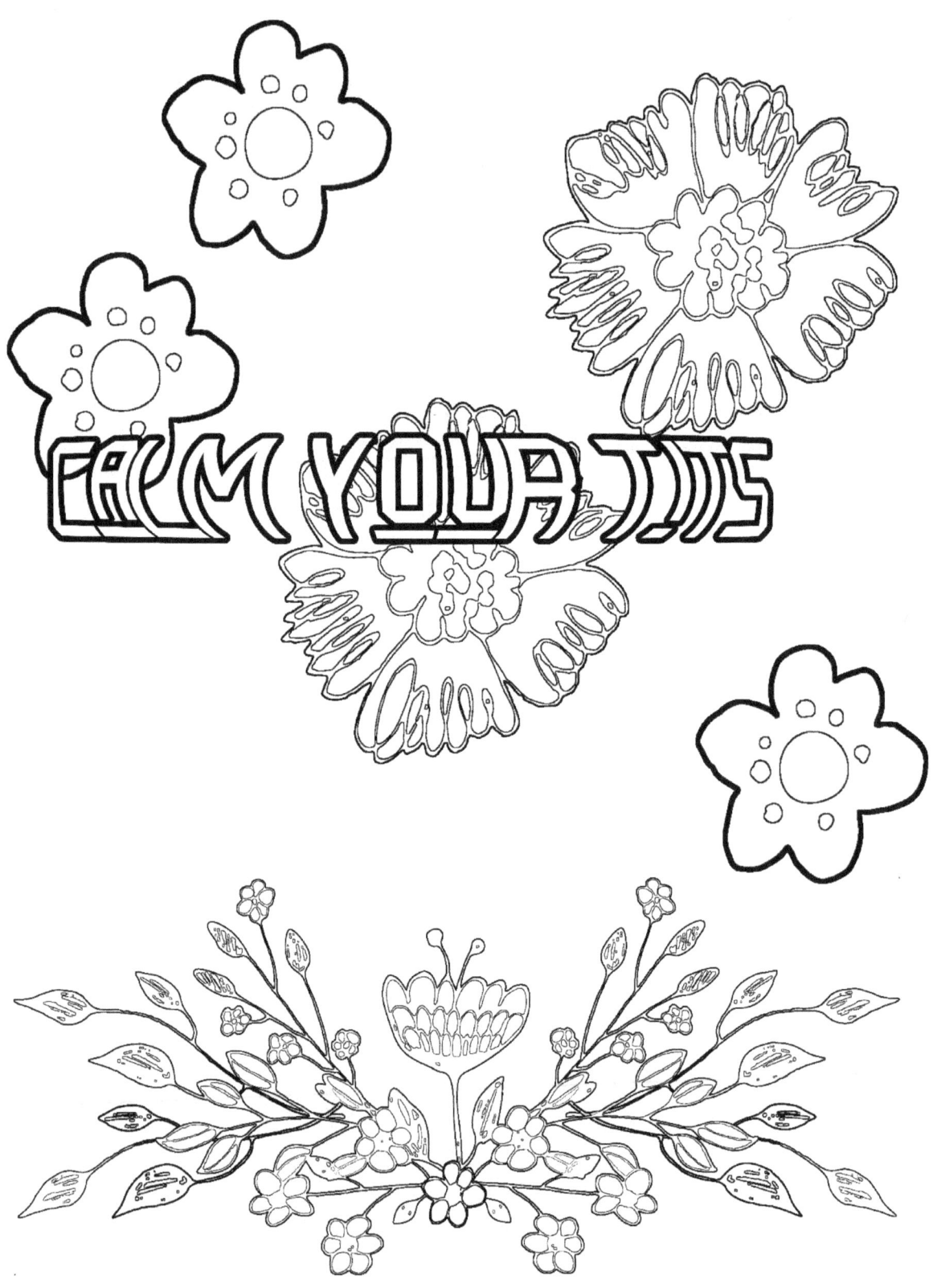

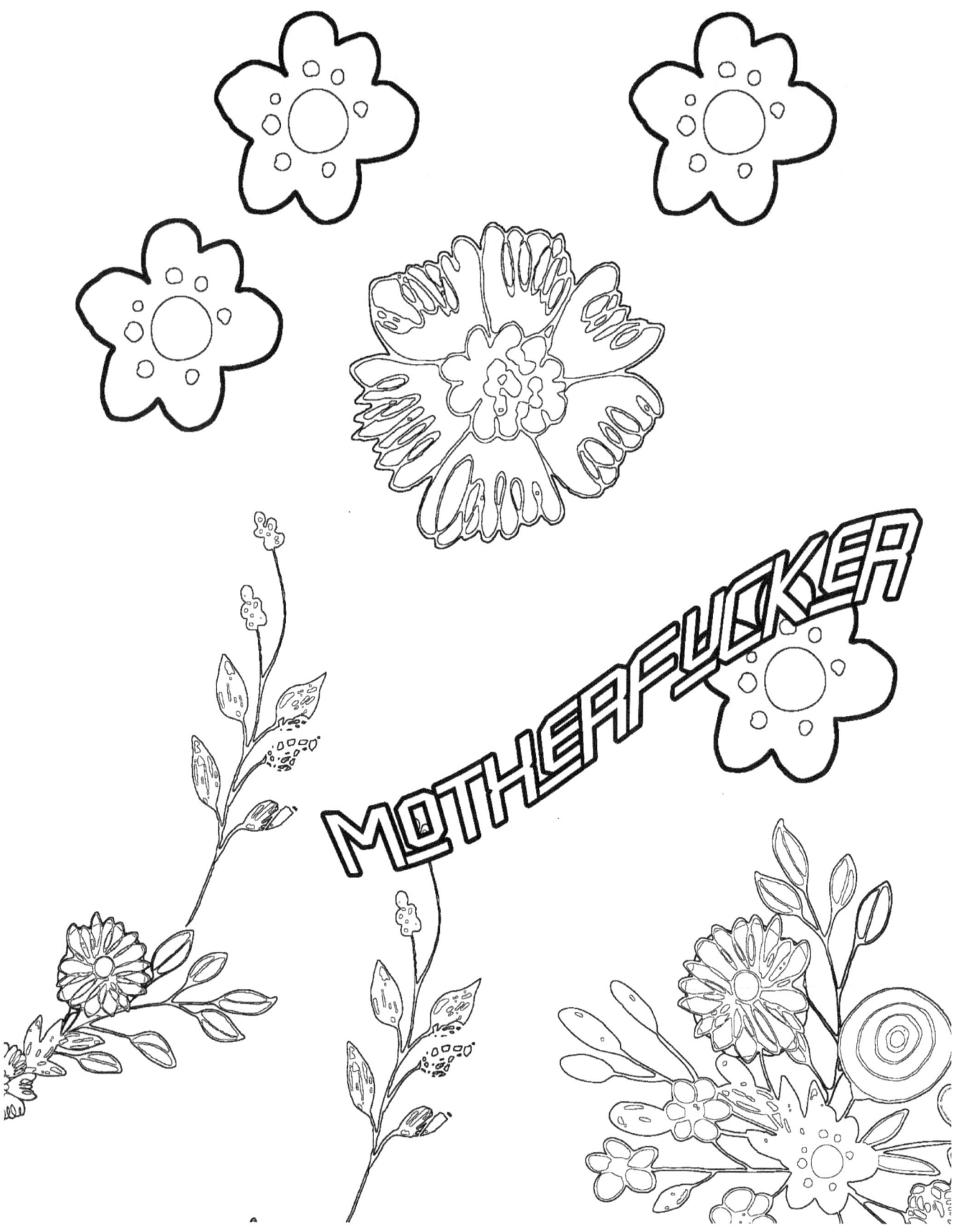

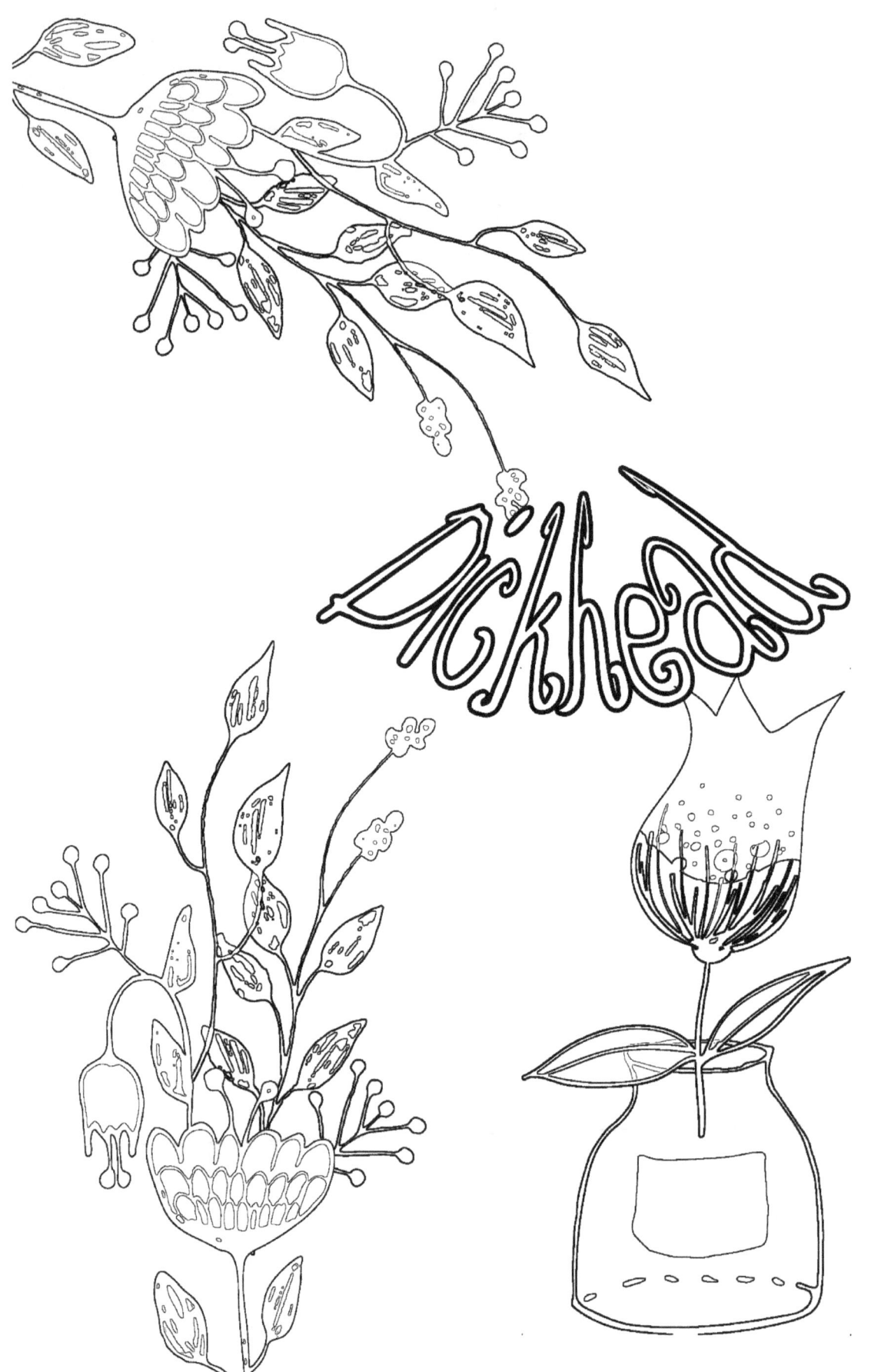

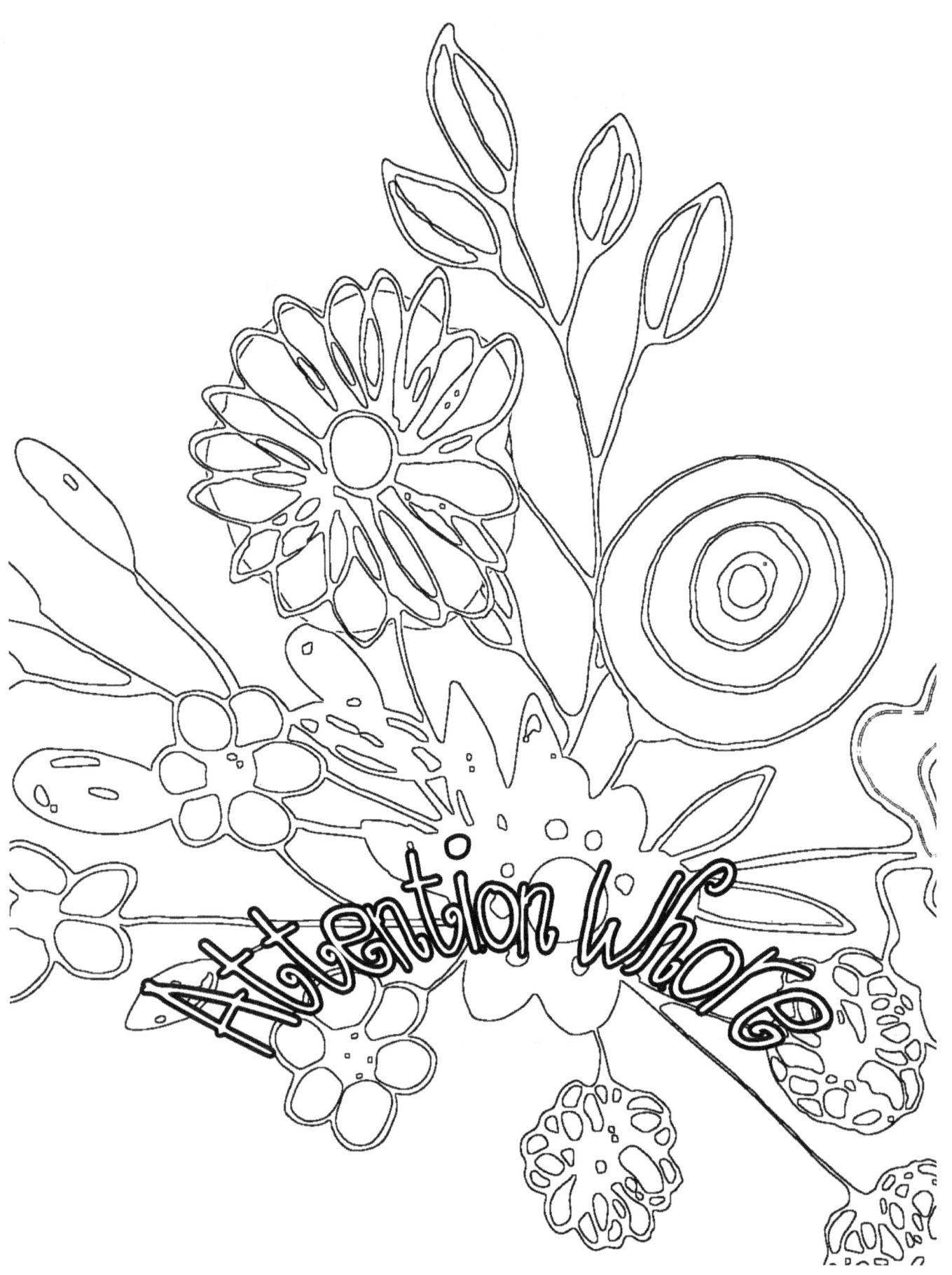

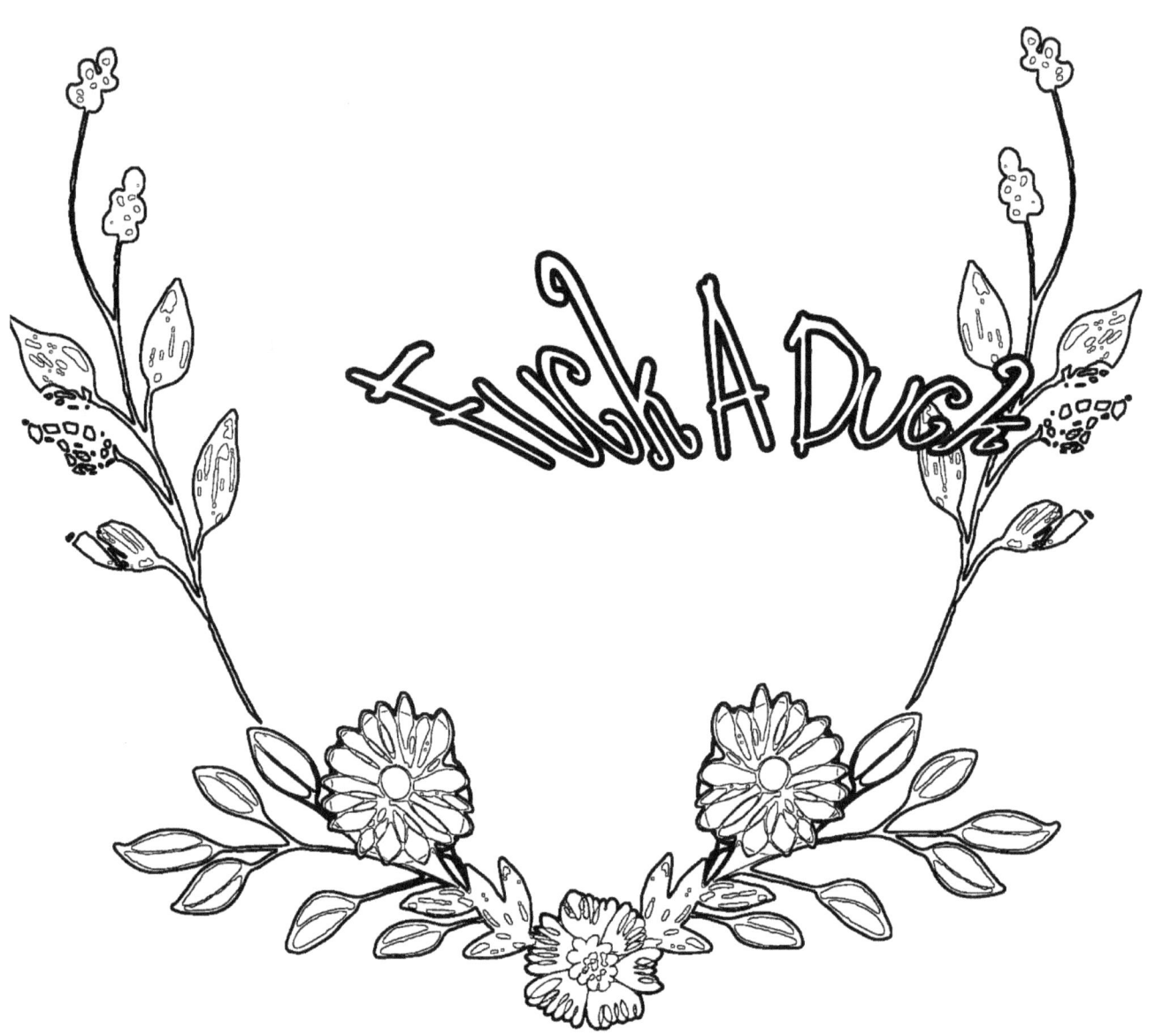

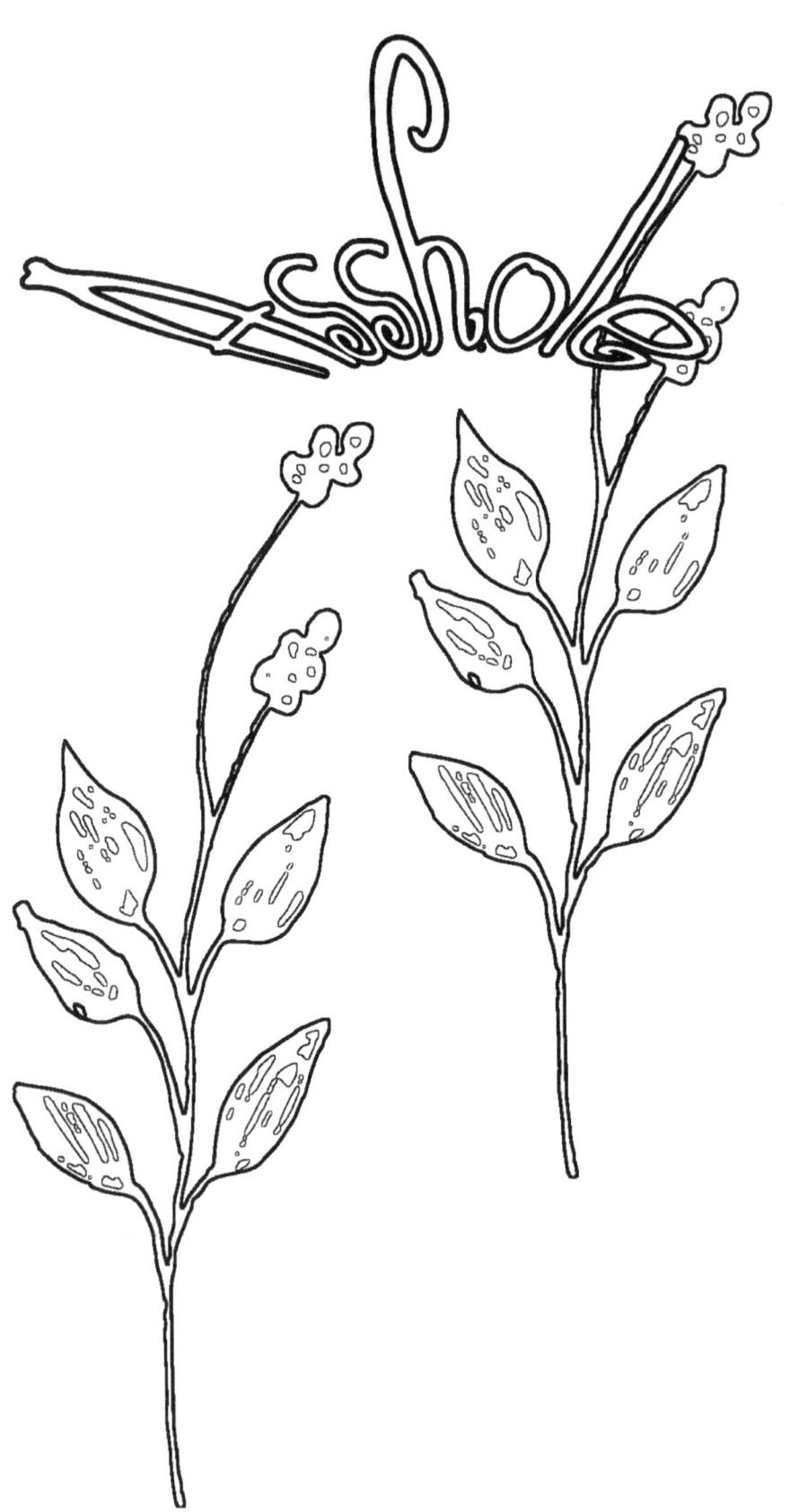

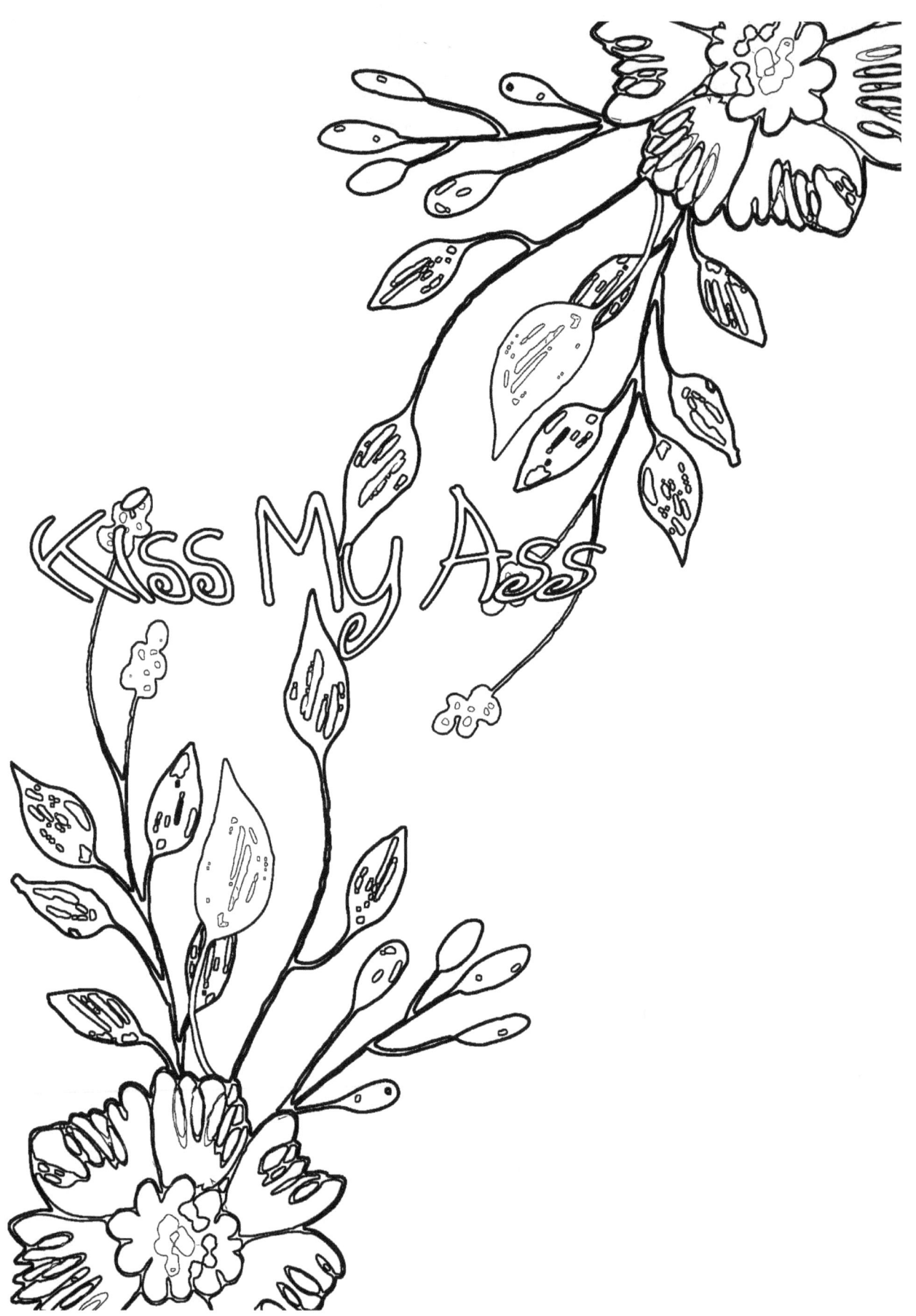

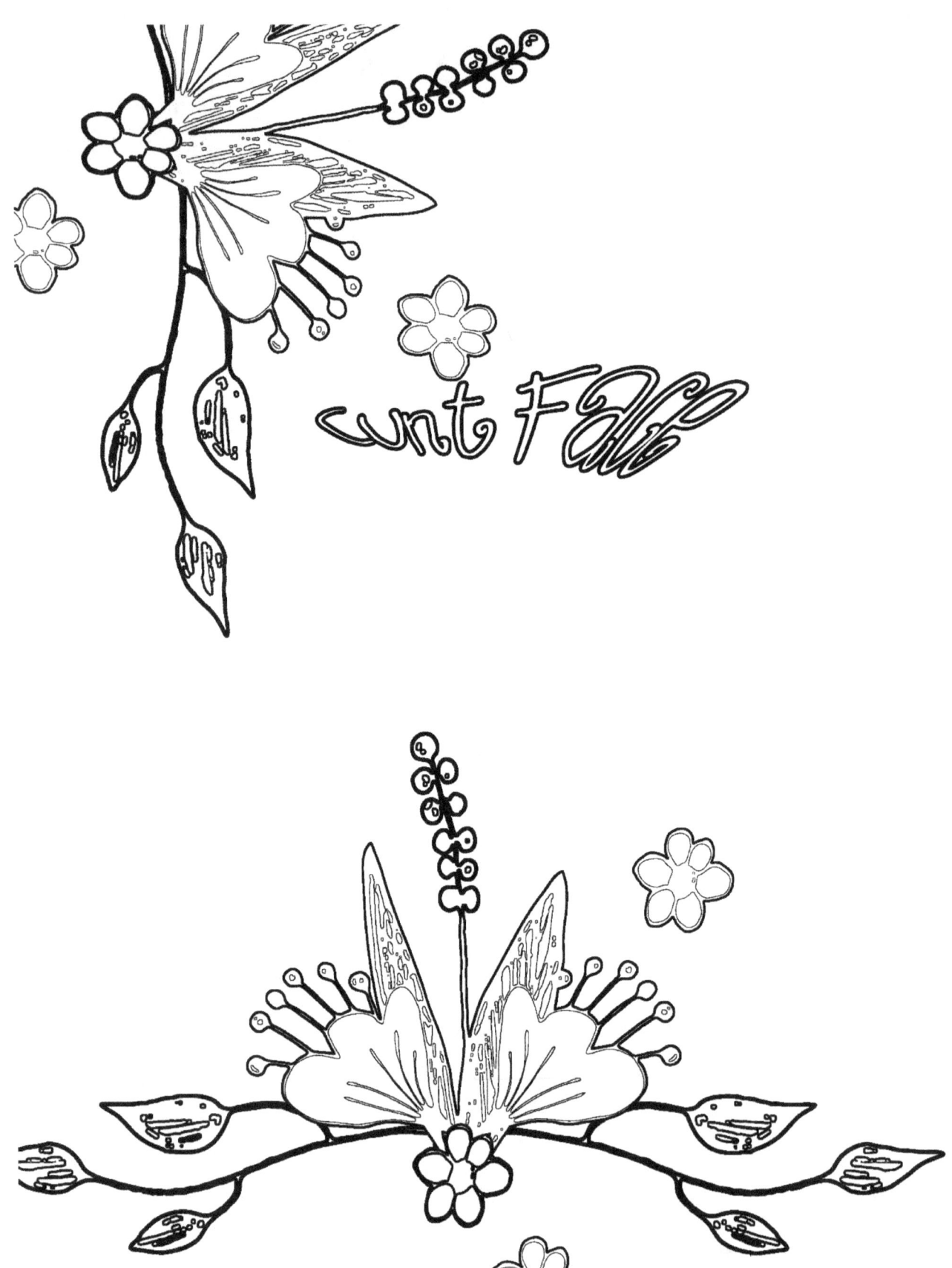

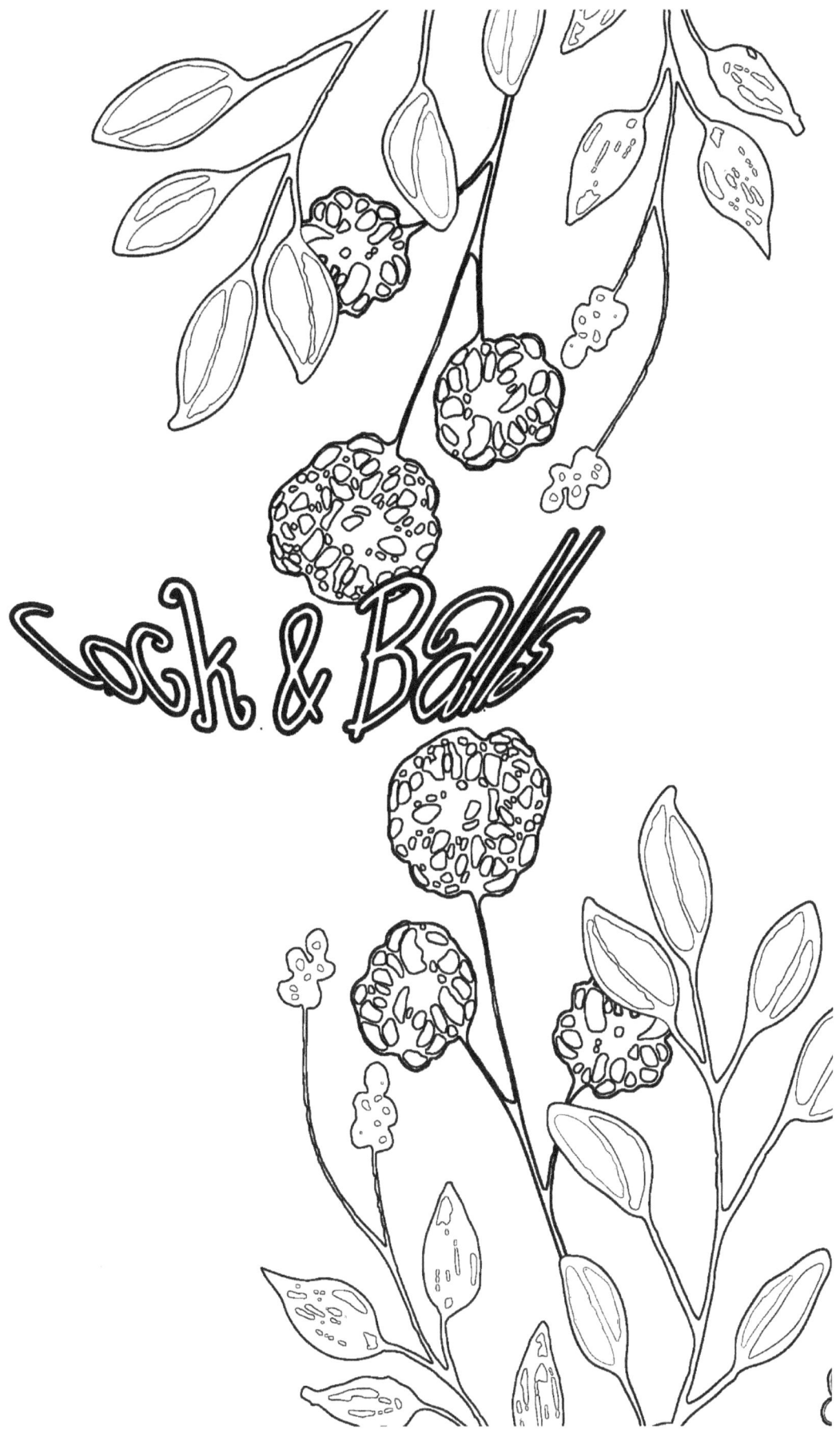

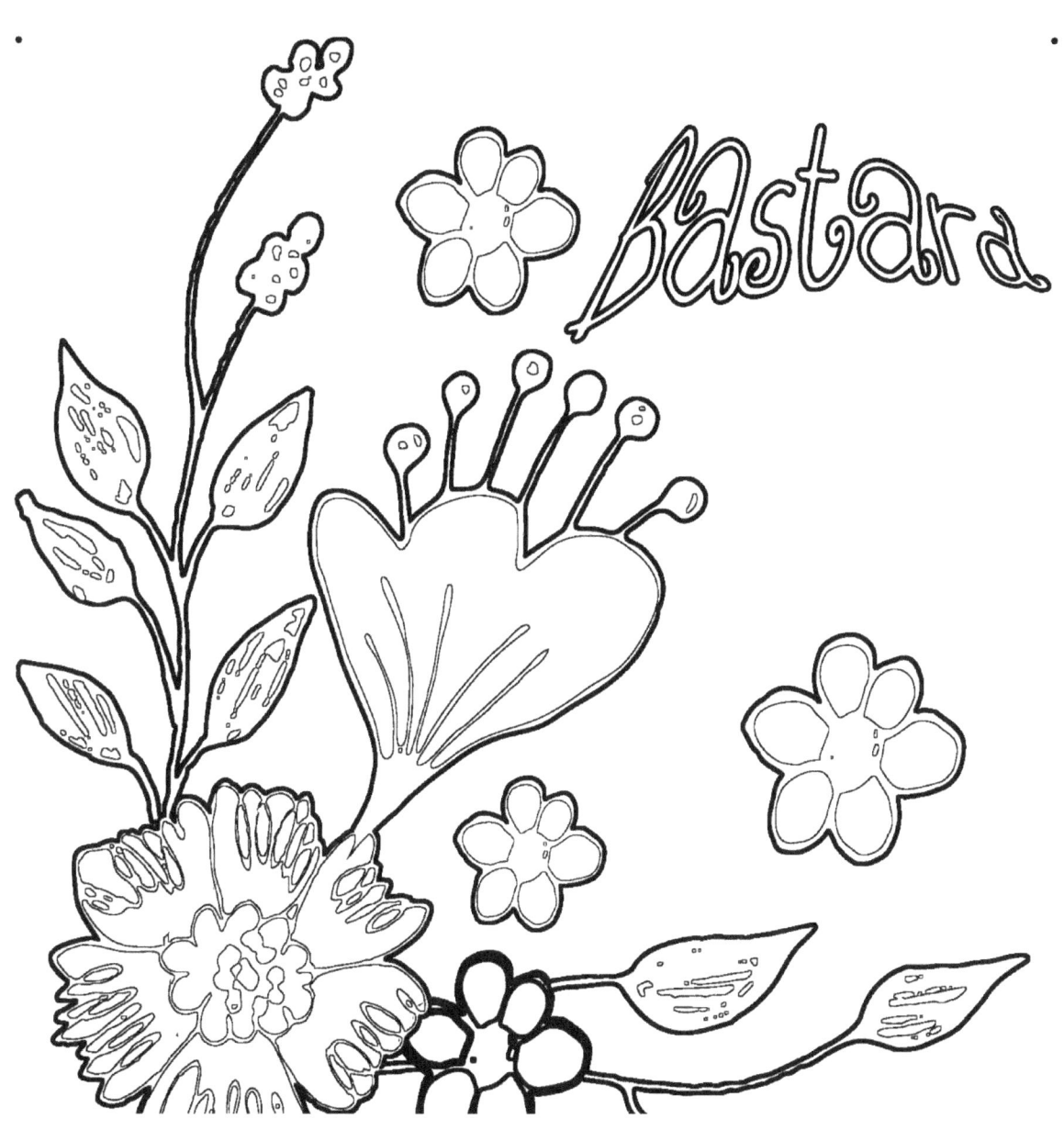

Bastard

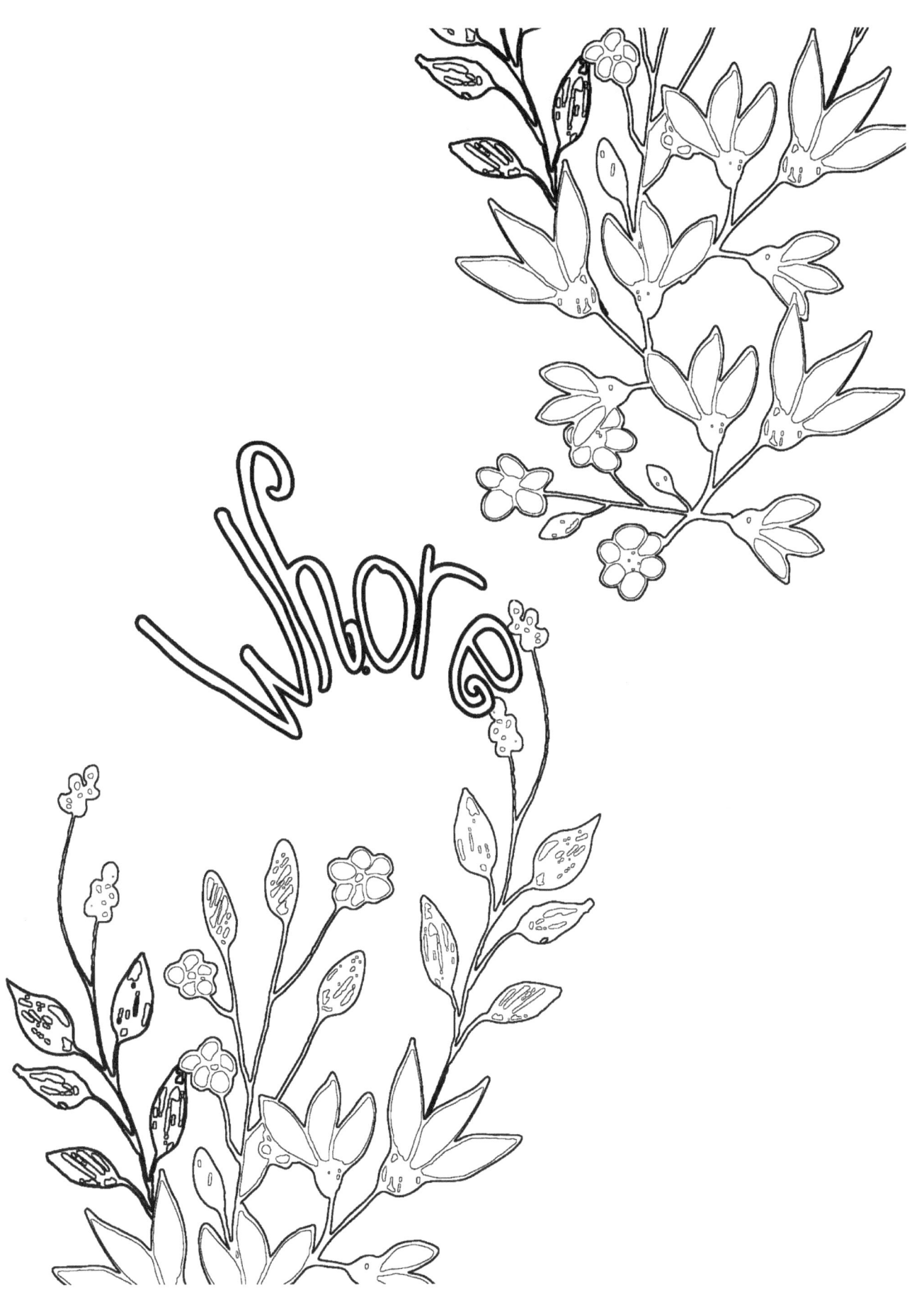

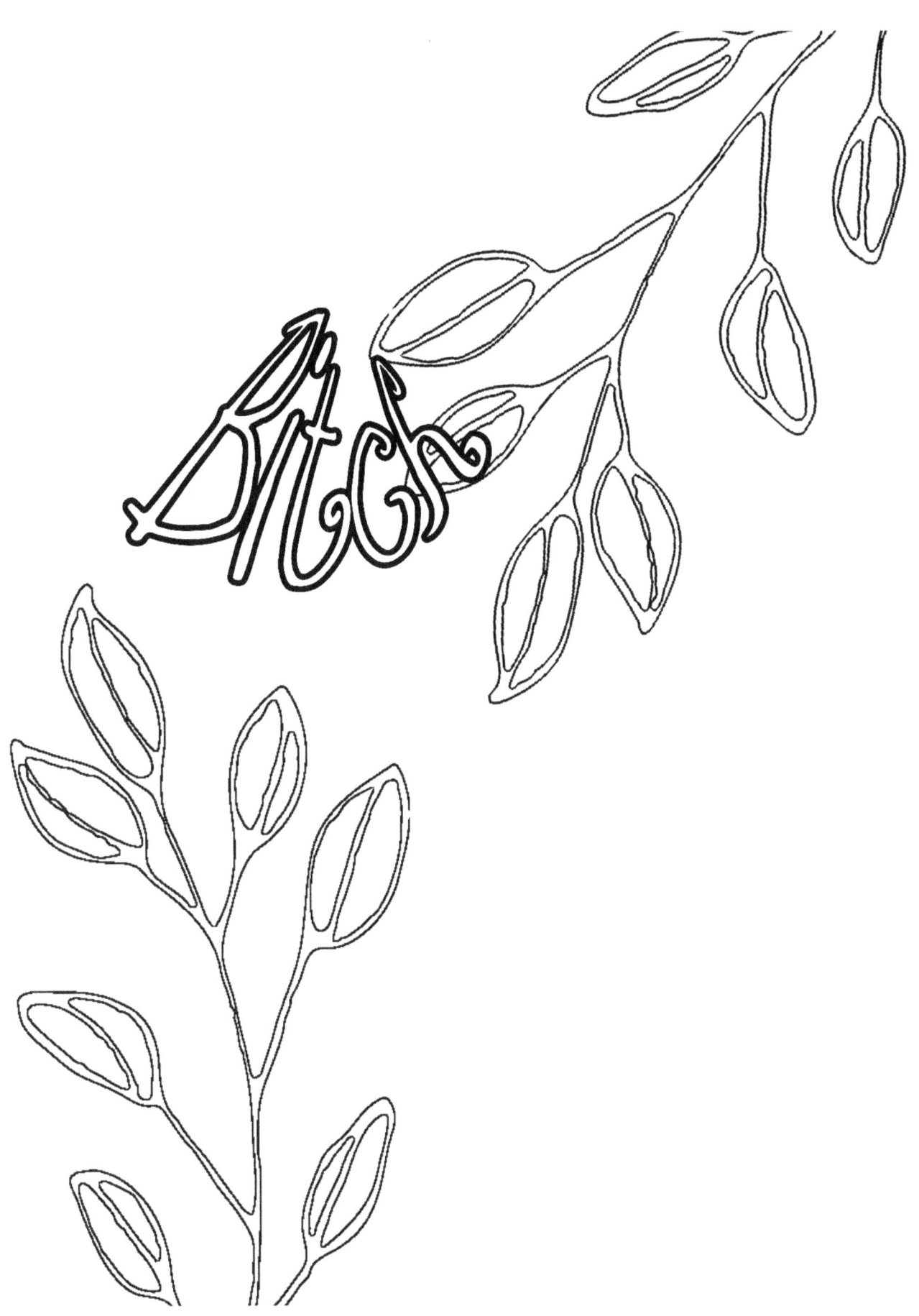

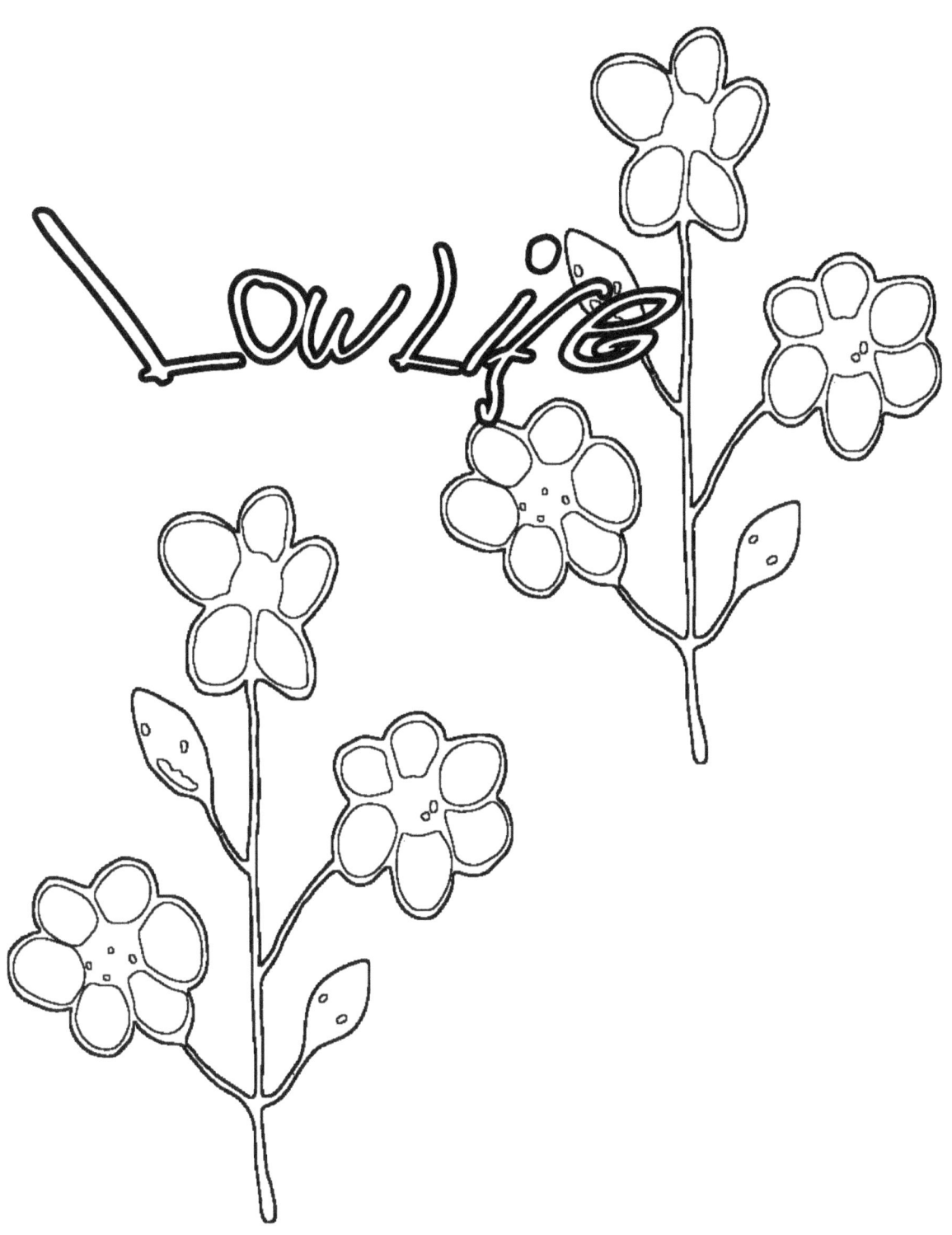

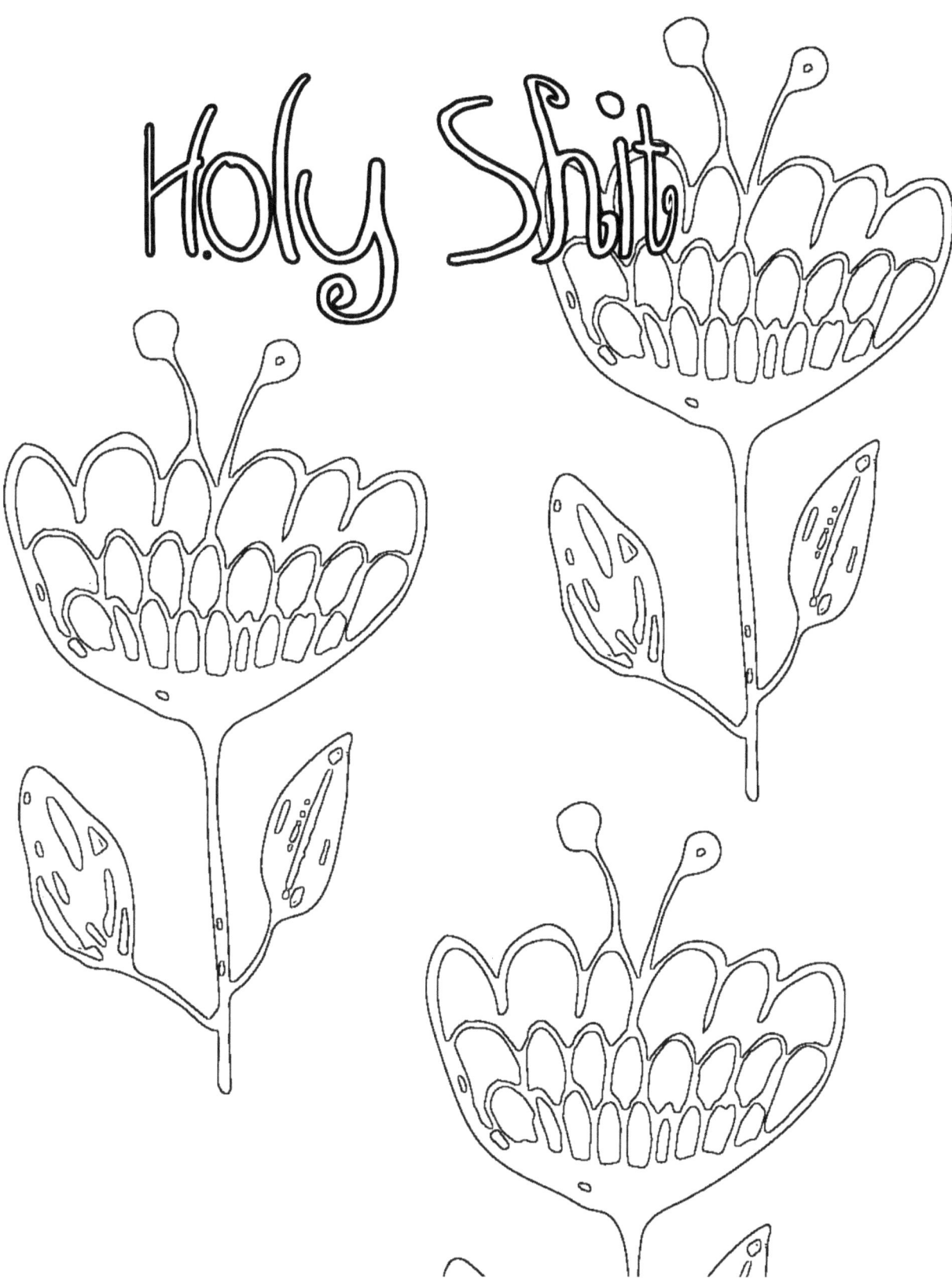

www.ingramcontent.com/pod-product-compliance
Lightning Source LLC
Chambersburg PA
CBHW081748170526
45167CB00009B/3962